The Power to
Overcome Crushing Seasons

The Power to
Overcome Crushing
Seasons

By:

Tammy L. Smith,
MSW, LSW

Please contact the author at the e-mail below for all permission, and speaking events at authortammysmith@outlook.com

All scriptures are taken from "The Holy Bible. New Living Translation copyright© 1996, 2004, 2007, 2013. Use for reference and quotes.

Scripture quotations marked MSG are taken from The Message, copyright © 1993, 2002, 2018. Use for reference and quotes.

Scripture quotations marked TPT are from The Passion Translation®. Copyright © 2017, 2018, 2020. Use for reference and quotes.

Scripture's quotations marked ESV are from The Holy Bible, English Standard Version (ESV) © 2001. Use for reference and quotes.
All definitions used are taken from Oxford Dictionary and Merriam-Webster.

Good news bible: The Good News Translation (GNT), formerly called the Good News Bible or Today's English Version, was first published as a full Bible in 1976 by the American Bible Society as a "common language" Bible.

Published in the United States
Right Side Publishing
Cover design by Don Smith
Editor Namra Ashraf
Editor Felicia S. Cauley

The Power to Overcome Crushing Seasons
ISBN- 9781955050463
Library of Congress number- 2024923917

Dedication

I dedicate this book to my children and
grandchildren. We are overcomers
in Christ Jesus.

Table of Contents

Foreword

The Power to Overcoming Crushing Seasons is a must-read. The life story and journey of the author, Tammy L. Smith, is a powerful sequence of events that must be shared with the world. She reminds us that during crushing seasons we need to keep moving forward because every situation in our life can be used to strengthen our purpose and assignment.

As an educator, dean, professor emerita, minister, and grieving mother of an only child who passed away at the age of nineteen, I found myself wanting to know how the author has navigated crushing events in her life. I have always been impressed with the author's level of confidence, tenacity, fortitude, Christian faith, and maturity. I did not know the details about her journey that led her to become the woman I and many others see and admire today. She does not look like what she has been through. The author allows the reader to revisit key personal events in her childhood and life.

We often hear terms like dysfunctional families, and Tammy Smith gives the reader concrete examples of what this looks like and ways to stop it, and she gives detailed guidance on coping through this process. She also provides a great illustration of what it means to be "crushed" that is insightful and powerful. Smith shares three steps that occurred while she was crushed beyond recognition: recognizing, admitting, and moving into action. Her discussion of blind spots provides the readers with practical strategies for moving forward during their crushing journey.

In addition, she provides tools and encouragement, as well as supportive information that will not only empower others but also transform them no matter where they are in the crushing process. Sharing the very intimate experience of her daughter's passing and how she survived this crushing season is tear-jerking and moving as she allows the reader to join her as she recounts this experience. The vivid visual examples help the reader to understand how others can survive grief as well as other crushing situations in their life. Throughout the chapters, Smith provides opportunities for the reader to explore and talk about what they have read as they personally reflect on the author's stories, practical examples, and strategies. Her life experiences, educational knowledge, work expertise, and Christian faith are strategically and gracefully woven together within the pages of this book. I encourage whoever reads The Power to Overcome Crushing Seasons to read with the expectation that their life WILL change as they read each page AND be prepared to receive the power to OVERCOME crushing seasons in their life!

Jennifer Faison Kelly, Ph.D.
Education Professor Emerita Capital
University- Columbus, OH
Founder & Educational Consultant, Train
Up A Child Intergenerational, LLC - Bowie, MD
Minister, Network of Local Churches,
Inc. – Columbus, OH

Introduction

The Power to Overcome Crushing Seasons was written with YOU in mind. The goal of the book is to provide YOU with tools, encouragement, and supportive information to empower you in crushing seasons. In this book, YOU will see how having a little hope can empower you to endure whatever season in YOUR life that is causing any type of discomfort and pain.

Also, inside this power-packed book, you will read about my *personal journey* and experience with family dysfunction, grief, and trauma. Therefore, for family and friends who dare to journey in the process with me and read through these anointed pages, remember, this is MY personal journey, and I am grateful to give you just a peak of what I have experienced. The hope is that while you are journeying through each story and illustration, you will perhaps see some parts of your own story and be inspired.

There are several stories related to my life and examples of experiencing life's painful crushing, as well as overcoming and walking in victory. Therefore, you may be triggered and or feel an emotional response to what is written in the pages to follow. If this happens, you may want to consider seeking a counselor to help you navigate through your own emotions and or stir up some things that were considered resolved. When you do so, STOP, BREATHE, and WRITE.

There will be a symbol of a **gem** provided throughout the book to let you know that this is a good time to *Review* and *Reflect* due to the level of intensity of the information shared.

My hope is that you will be both empowered and inspired to keep moving forward in your purpose. You were born with the ability to overcome every obstacle in your way or whatever season of crushing you are in. You can overcome it!

Acknowledgements

First, I give honor and thanks to my Lord and Savior, Jesus Christ, for blessing me with strength and Grace to complete this book; I could not have done this without Him. Next, I want to express my appreciation to my husband, Don, for his prayers, support, and encouragement.

Thank you to my parents for loving me, giving me life, and demonstrating the *power to overcome*!!

Thank you to Bishop Scales and the Rhema Christian Center Family for being an essential part of my journey by helping me to discover and deploy my gifts and talents. Also, I want to give a special thank you to my spiritual mother, Beverly Moore, for providing wise counsel, love, and guidance.

Lastly, thank you to everyone who has been an integral part of my journey and to all of those who provided empathetic listening.

CHAPTER 1

How it all began...

Before we dive deep into how it all began, I want you to be prepared as we transition from the earlier days of my life to later experiences. This journey will help you understand the formation of my strengths and how you can use my insights to develop and strengthen yours.

My story begins with the early times when my mother and I lived with my grandmother. During this time, there were multiple family members living in the home and I can remember our family being close-knit supporting each other. I remember sneaking and drinking grandmother's cold glass of ice water in a jar. This was the best water I have ever tasted! My mother was a loving, kind person and the Matriarch of our family. She was the one who brought several family members together in caring ways. The love my mother had for others is something I will never forget! She loved people past their flaws, faults, and shortcomings. Now, that is the kind of love we all need! Unconditional!

My mother often put her love on display by allowing loved ones to live with us. She was truly benevolent and would open our door often to others. One season, my relative came to live with us and as usual, mother showed her love and immense support to him. On my way to school one winter morning, I saw him trying to get his passed-out girlfriend into the house. Can you imagine the thoughts that were running through my mind and how deeply this affected me as a middle schooler trying to catch the bus to school? I went out with my mother to help him pull her up a slippery snowy hill and get her in; her weight against the slippery snow made things hard, but we managed to bring her in the house. There were similar instances and memories of family enjoying themselves until the wee hours of the morning while I was getting ready for school.

This was considered normal for me: to wake up for school and people still partying.

 **How was your upbringing? Do you have any significant events that come to mind that were life-altering?**

While being in the care of a sitter at the age of twelve years old, there were plenty of opportunities to both drink beer and smoke cigarettes. The sitter was a disciplinarian; however, she allowed me and the other child in her care to try her beer. I remember it like it was yesterday, Budweiser with a sprinkle of salt. The sitter would give us a little tiny glass, and guess what? We enjoyed every bit of it, not knowing it was a setup for things to come. Also, whenever she walked out of the room, leaving her lit cigarette in the ashtray, the other kids and I would take puffs.

As time went on, I became old enough to stay home alone, get myself ready for middle school, and go to the bus stop without any company. However, one chilly winter morning, I stumbled across a bottle of liquor in the kitchen cabinet. I am sure you know what happened next. Yes, I began to experiment with alcohol and would take a shot before I went to school. It became a regular routine to the point of putting water in the bottle to make sure my mother did not notice anything missing. I became skilled at measuring how much I took out and would replace it with water, but I was still worried she would find out someday. As a child, like most, I was curious, and my curiosity led me to want to know what it tasted like. Little did I know that what started as a little taste would change into a habit that brought great pain to my life and others.

The culminating events led me to a life of addiction, mismanagement, and family dysfunction. The dysfunction continued in my life, and I was pregnant with my first child at 17 years of age. By the time I was 22, I had three beautiful children I love! However, my lack of knowledge and parenting skills, along with influences from alcohol and cocaine addiction, increased the dysfunction in my household.

 **Can you think of habits that manifested later in life that may have started when you were a child or due to family dysfunction?**

Family Dysfunction

What is the cycle of dysfunction, and how to break this cycle? *"Dysfunctional families are characterized by multiple conflicts, tense relationships, chaos, neglect, abuse, poor communication, lack of empathy and secrecy to an extent that the emotional and physical needs of the family members are not met, especially children"* *(Mphaphuli, 2023).* Therefore, when talking about dysfunction, this means we are repeating the cycle described in this definition. I saw dysfunction on many levels in my family at a young age.

In families where things are out of sync, bringing about change requires a strong desire and a firm decision to make it happen. God has called many of us to be the change agent, deliverer, and chain breaker to break the cycle. For me, the process began with baby steps. At first, I accepted that my life was a mess and I needed help from outside of the dysfunctional circle of friends and family.

One day, I looked in the mirror and saw someone and deep down, I knew this person was not me. I wanted something different and took the steps to make the change. Little did I know that one step would give me a life free of addiction and its lifestyle because it came with a cost! I wanted nothing more than to break the dysfunctional cycle and give my family a loving, healthy, and caring environment. I wanted *"A positive atmosphere within the family, open communication, strong interpersonal relationships between parents and children, harmony and cohesion, and everything that contributes to a conducive and a safe space for children to develop healthy habits" (Mphaphuli, 2023)*, which is described as a healthy functioning family.

On November 11th, 1993, I walked five miles to a treatment center after hitting rock bottom, losing my dignity and respect, and feeling helpless and hopeless. Before I walked in, I could hear a small voice *nudging* me to say, "Help me, Jesus." The next thing I knew, I was standing inside the building. I was later sent to a facility for detox, and then to a two-year treatment program for women and children. I attended many counseling sessions, with a gamut of emotions and expressions of those emotions. I had to learn how to live, be a parent, pay bills, and become a responsible adult. Those were my first steps towards freedom, but it came with a desire to make a change. I wanted something different and took the steps to make the change. The change continued in my family when I witnessed my mother getting baptized and my father committing his life to the Lord and joining the Church as a minister of music. I was blessed to visit the house of our Lord with both of my parents; our faith in religion had been restored through the power of the Cross and the Resurrection of Jesus Christ.

 **When change is needed, we often receive internal signals that something is off or needs to shift. Have you experv ienced this?**

Family dysfunction is nothing new, and many individuals are experiencing some of it even today. The Bible also discusses this topic at the beginning of Genesis 3:6 (NIV): *When the woman saw that the fruit of the tree was good for food and pleasing to the eye, and desirable for gaining wisdom, she took some and ate it. She also gave some to her husband, who was with her, and he ate it.* This act opened the door to sin and family dysfunction. I John 2:16 (NIV) clearly explains the conflicts of mankind and their downfall in the following verse: "For everything in the world—the lust of the flesh, the lust of the eyes, and the pride of life—comes not from the Father but from the world." So, now we understand that dysfunction might not have started with you, but it definitely can end with you! We cannot change our past, but we can shape and change our future...one step at a time, one prayer at a time...and one process at a time.

Change began for me when I gave my life to the Lord. I've learned that some things are a process due to generational strongholds and the power of choice, because my middle daughter would later struggle with some of the same issues. Even my middle daughter struggled with addiction and mental illness. At 14 years old, she began to run away and got into the wrong crowd. I would later have to file a petition with the courts to help me keep her safe, in school, and to cover myself due to the truancy laws. As a young adult, she was in an abusive relationship and one time had to jump out of a second-floor window to escape her abuser. My daughter struggled with untreated mental illness, addiction, and abuse. I did everything in my power to help her as much as possible. If you know how the cycle of addiction works, you will understand it's simply that…a cycle, if untreated, and continued connections with old people and places remain the same. I will talk more about this as we move into Chapter 3.

Journal

CHAPTER 2

Crushed Beyond Recognition

In this chapter, we will talk about being crushed beyond recognition. When I say crushed, I mean something being smashed to the point of being un-recognizable. I take this crushing similar to a car that is towed to the junkyard waiting to be crushed in a trash compactor. However, did you know that crushed cars are recycled and can be used again? This is because the car was built with precious metals that still have value (remember this point),but without crushing the car, it's left sitting, taking up space in someone's garage, or better yet, on the street. There-fore, the car, though it appears to have reached its full potential and purpose for being created, is crushed, used again, and perhaps in a different capacity from the one used before the crushing.

If you have witnessed the crushing of a car in a compactor, you would know the ruins and mess that's left behind. Just as the crushing of a car is a harsh visual, even though it has no connections to emotions, the crushing blows in life are equally devastating. However, as humans, we think, "How much more of this crushing can we take," or "Surely this is it," or "How will I ever recover from this." The answer is you can, and you will recover! We will talk more about this in the last few chapters.

 **Are you experiencing a form of crushing and feeling utterly hopeless?**

Like the car, I experienced crushing beyond recognition. Just as a car built with precious metals, you and I are made with the precious image of our Master and Savior Jesus Christ. Genesis 1:27NLT states: "*So God created human beings in his own image. In the image of God, he created them; male and female, He created them.*" We were created with intricate details that only the Master could put together. He also created us with a purpose in mind, and the purpose is oftentimes birthed through a fine-tuning process. It's like when you hand me a guitar. No matter how I strum the chords as a non-musician, the sound will be awful until a guitarist fine-tunes it. The guitarist knows exactly how much stretching and pulling of the strings are required to make the guitar *produce the sound* it was created to produce. Consequently, God knows what is needed in our lives to *produce a sound* on the earth that will draw people to him.

Our Heavenly Father is not sitting around waiting for opportunities to crush us or cause us pain, but He makes it work for us! Romans 8:28 NIV says, *"All things work together for the good of them that love God and are called according to his purpose."* It's about purpose, and we will talk more about this in Chapter 5...but right now, let's continue the conversation about Crushed beyond recognition.

One day, while in the store, I ran into someone that I spent time with when I was steep in the lifestyle of addiction. When I went up to him, he did not recognize me. He took a moment to stare at me and then said, "Tammy, I did not recognize who you were." Then the next words were, "You got saved, didn't you." And, of course, my answer was "YES." While sharing this story with you, my heart was filled with joy and gladness, and I even chuckled while thinking about this part of my life. See, what I realize is somewhere along my transformation, my journey (yes, a journey), I became unrecognizable, but for the better. I also realize that it took years to get to this place, and it did not happen overnight.

I had to *put in the work* to go from dysfunctional to functional because I was desperate for change. Now, I took that same desperation to move toward change, and I was willing to do whatever was required of me. See, I remember walking around with a broken leg in a cast, going places to feed an addiction. There were times when I walked in the rain…it did not matter. I was desperate! I was so desperate I did not care about ruining my cast; it got wet and dirty, and I did not care whether my leg healed properly or not. Why? Because I was desperate for change and willing to do whatever was required to move towards a healthier way of living. Because of that desperation, my life is now a testimony unto Jesus.

 **How desperate are you to bring a positive change in your life? What steps are you willing to take to move towards that change?**

Put In the Work

Going from a dysfunctional life to a functional life is not easy. It takes hard work, dedication, perseverance, and determination to make the necessary changes to live a different way. I had to **RAM,** which is the acronym for <u>r</u>ecognize, <u>a</u>dmit, and <u>m</u>ove into action. The word Ram has various meanings according to Merriam Webster; however, the ones that speak to the process are: "a warship with a heavy beak at the prow for piercing an enemy ship... any of various guided pieces for exerting pressure or for driving or forcing something by impact" (2024). Also, the Bible speaks of a Ram in the bush in Genesis 22:13 (NIV). God *provided* a ram in the bush for Abraham as a test of his obedience. Therefore, for context and purpose, the steps are used to power through and break through barriers of dysfunction. RAM is a provision to equip, empower, and give you the tools needed to break every barrier of dysfunction in your life. So, let's prepare to power through and press through by breaking the enemies' lies and deceit to freedom.

Recognize

Recognizing a need to change can be extremely difficult if we cannot see that a change is needed. However, there are times when things are glaring in our lives, and it is obvious that a change needs to take place or something devastating will happen. I will say that I had high hopes for my life and I would contribute that to my relationship with my mother as well as perhaps being a firstborn, a natural born leader and just the God prompting that I had within to know that there was something greater. A friend I knew from elementary school said, "You were always a leader; you were just leading the wrong way." Perhaps it was the way of the Lord; His purpose, His plan, and gift instilled in me gave me the will to change and live a better way. Also, there are times when this recognition comes from someone else because it's hard to see the truth when we are blind to it. These are called Blind Spots.

Let's discuss the blind spots in cars. When changing lanes on busy roads, it's your mirrors or the passenger sitting next to you that can provide assistance to aid in keeping you safe. The mirror and people in your car help you to see what you cannot see. There are areas in the car that are unseen, even with mirrors, making it difficult to switch lanes... so we proceed with caution. The same goes for the blind spots in our lives; individuals who love and care about us can typically see them and let us know so that we do not wreck ourselves. People outside of us can see them very well, and it is a blessing to have those types of people in our lives. So, when people around you are telling you that you have a problem, then chances are you have something that needs to be addressed. Similarly, to watching a movie you've watched before, the next time you watch it, you typically see something different. I find it interesting when this happens, and it's almost shocking, like, "Why didn't I see that the first time." I believe the answer to the question is capacity, which is the maximum amount of something that can be contained *(Oxford Dictionary)*.

Our ability to perceive things is limited by time and our capacity to take in information. We can't grasp everything happening in a single moment, so this really comes down to our capacity. We can say that the Holy Spirit and people can show us what we need to see. The Holy Spirit, however, can show us what we need to see, and he uses other people in our lives to help us as well. The Holy Spirit, also known as our helper, has the capacity to see everything. Because the Holy Spirit is God and God is everywhere present. He knows all, and he sees all and so through the power of the Holy Spirit, we can develop discernment and be in tune with the things in our lives that simply are not pleasing to God. In *John 14:26 ESV, it is written* "But the Helper, the Holy Spirit, whom the Father will send in my name, he will teach you all things and bring to your remembrance all that I have said to you."

There is a Serenity prayer that says: "God grants me the Serenity to accept the things I cannot change, and the courage to change the things I can, and the wisdom to know the difference" (Reinhold Niebuhr 1930). This is a prayer that we can ask the Lord to show us, help us change things, and allow us to accept the things that only He can change. We cannot change others; we can only change ourselves!

Admit

Admit has two meanings: "confess to be true and to allow someone to enter a space" (*Oxford Dictionary*). I will speak in the context of both definitions as they apply to this step in the journey to change. The hard part was to recognize the need to bring change in life, now admitting it is even more challenging. Whenever you are trying to bring improvement to your life, remember if you're not desperate enough, you won't push yourself to make it happen. There is power in admitting!

When I talk about admitting, I mean someone saying, "Yes, it was me," and by saying yes it was me, there is liberty and freedom in those few words. Also, the power of confession and confessing one's shortcomings has the ability to not only set you free but set others free. I had to admit something was wrong and I had to submit myself to the urge of bringing change in my life. I had to admit that the life I was living was not in alignment with the actual plans God had for me. The call and the purpose of my life were greater than the dysfunction, and the dysfunction had to cease and desist; so that the glory of God could be revealed through His vessel. In I John 1:19 NIV, the scripture speaks of this step: *"If we **confess** our sins, he is faithful and just and will forgive us our sins and purify us from all unrighteousness."*

The key word in the scripture text is **confess**! If we **confess,** admit, and acknowledge we have sinned, meaning missed the mark or did something wrong, we reap the benefits of doing so… we receive forgiveness and purity and seal the deal with our relationship with our Heavenly Father. It takes a level of maturity and responsibility to make a confession and admit when you have made a mistake, and oftentimes, the flesh does not want to bow down and say, "I'm sorry, I was wrong…

taking ownership of one's mistake is a sign of maturity!"

Exposure is the key to freedom! When you expose yourself, you do not have to worry about someone else exposing you! For the admitting step, I recommend the following prayer to prepare you for the next step: "Lord, I admit I have done wrong, I have (name it), and now I want to be led by you so I can live a life pleasing to you. Show me the way." By asking to be shown the way, you have made an open invitation for the Lord to come in, which brings us to the second part of the meaning of admit...to allow someone in. When admitting, I am saying I've tried it my way, and now I need to try life another way. To do this, I had to let people in my life lead me, guide me, and show me the way. Some of those people were counselors, coaches, pastors, mentors, and of course, my Lord and Savior. After such a request, I had to move into action!

Move Into Action

You may ask why *move into action*? My response is how does one change without doing something? Change requires action, movement, and consistency.

Drastic change requires drastic measures, so if you want change, and it's something that significant, you must do something significant to make that change… And that's what I did.

One of the things that I did to move into action is to receive counseling, which began when my children and I lived in a place called Amethyst: housing for women who are going through treatment from addictions. I was a part of that program for a little over two years, and during that time, I received intensive therapy throughout the day. I had accountability partners and sponsors, and I was able to address some of the dysfunctions in my life.

While going through this intense process, I began to mend my relationship with God. It was through this relationship and program that I began to develop a prayer life. One thing I remember is that during my recovery, I was told to find a higher power. As a kid, I remember going to church periodically, and the only higher power I knew was Jesus. I began talking to him daily because I wanted to be free and live a different life.

As I became closer to the Lord, I knew I had to rethink my life decisions and choose a path for myself. Do I continue this journey with the Amethyst program or do I step out on Faith and dedicate my life to God? At this time, I had a conversation with my sponsor, and I told her I feel like the Lord is calling me and I need to make a decision in terms of my commitment to attending meetings or if I'm going to give myself fully to the Lord and go to church in the place of those meetings? To my surprise, she had a very supportive response and suggested that I should follow God's will. Each person's walk is unique. I've seen individuals who attended both meetings and church. However, that wasn't the path the Lord chose for me. Therefore, I decided to move in the direction provided for me.

I started attending Church with my children, we were all baptized and committed our new life to God's way. We went to a youth revival and got baptized with the Holy Spirit during worship service with my hands up to the Lord, surrendering all I knew about life and desiring Him. The next thing I knew, I felt like my feet were lifted off the ground, and I began to speak in my heavenly language as declared in the Book of Acts 10:44-46NKJV [44] While Peter was still speaking these words, the *Holy Spirit fell* upon all those who heard the word. [45] ...the gift of the Holy Spirit had been poured out... [46] For they heard them speak with tongues and magnify God.

This is just like our Heavenly Father: we may seek Him for one thing, but He knows exactly what else we need in our search. I wanted a change, and that night I felt transformed in a profound way. By God's grace and mercy, I have remained on the path to Christ.

Journal

_____

_____

_____

_____

_____

_____

_____

_____

_____

_____

_____

_____

_____

_____

_____

_____

_____

_____

_____

_____

_____

CHAPTER 3

Surviving the Crushing Season

One would think after overcoming drug addiction and breakthroughs in family dysfunction, life would be constant, healthy, and simply enjoyable without tragedy. What we must all know is that we will have challenges in our lives, some of which might be extremely painful. Especially the unexpected life blows that have the power to knock you off your feet and make you breathless! This is what happened to me…I had the wind knocked out of me!

The Crushing

In 2022, I started working on a job that best suited my life and purpose. During my training, I heard the devastating news that I wish upon no parent; it was about my middle child Patrice, who was 33 at the time, had passed. With shock, devastation, uncertainty, disbelief, and intense pain, I screamed out in my car as I drove to the location where she was found unresponsive. I remember driving there recklessly as I cried my heart out. I stopped at my spiritual mother's house first as I could not bear the idea of seeing her beautiful body lying cold on the ground. I cried out, "Why do I have to bury my child." I was torn, shocked, and felt *ambushed* because I had just spoken with her the night before, and she was packing to move to a new home.

Patrice began to hang with old company and ended up passing away by an accidental overdose of drugs that was laced with fentanyl. Everyone who knew and loved her was devastated and could not believe she was gone. The old friends she was with during her last breath abandoned her in a running car in front of her house. It was painful for me to share the details of her passing, especially the part where she had been lying still in a running car for hours, and no one was around her. My beautiful Patrice had no intention of leaving us at that time. Yet, another plan was unfolding-one that would shake me to my very core. My sweet baby girl had no plans of dying yet, and she wanted to live. However, destiny's work shook my very foundation. I felt our lives were *ambushed* by what felt like a surprise attack. This feeling left me depleted, despondent, and helpless. Needless to say, I was lost and confused since she and I spoke the night before.

I became concerned about her affairs and the thoughts crossed my mind if she had time to reconnect with God. Months later, I discovered she recommitted her life to the Lord and prayed the prayer of salvation. I'm grateful for the God-ordained encounter with one of her friends that shared the details of this confession. The Lord knew that this was important to me and had two other women in the faith call me to address my concerns. God knows, and he sent a total of three people to console me around my concern without me initiating any of those conversations. This is why I can say that I still believe and trust God, even after experiencing loss. He continues to be faithful and absolutely no one can tell me different.

As I continued to share a little more about the devastating blow of Patrice's death; when she was just two weeks old, she stopped breathing. I thought I lost her then, but through life-saving methods of CPR and divine help, I breathed life back into her. Now, here I am, 33 years later, lost and wondering if I could have gotten to her in time. I could have rescued her as I did before, so what was I to do next? I know I was trying my best not to lose my mind. What I did was tap into my instinct…fight. As a youngster, physical fighting was a way I expressed my anger. But this time, the battle was different. I had to fight in a different way, to survive and to cope with the devastating loss of one of my children—a fight unlike any I'd ever known.

 **Have you experienced feelings of being ambushed? This is a good place to take a moment to pause, breathe, reflect, and write.**

Surviving the Crushing

One of my favorite quotes from the movie Rocky Balboa (2006) is "Fighters fight" because that's who he was - a fighter. However, there are times when our approach to fighting needs to evolve, as our previous methods may end up causing more harm than good. For instance, someone new to swimming may initially try to stay afloat by flailing their arms. In such moments, it's important to recognize the vast power of the ocean (or problem) and choose to surrender. In learning how to swim, one of the first lessons is to flip over on your back and float in a position of surrender. Viewing this from a biblical standpoint, when we turn to the Lord for salvation, healing, and intervention, the initial step is to surrender to Him. Remember, you do not have to fight alone or do the minimum to survive. Just like the oceans current will pull you down and outweigh you, so will situations. We must trust God to keep us a float when things are unbearable. This is what I meant when I mentioned above that sometimes you have to give up on fighting because it is dangerous for your end goal, which is to survive.

 **What is your survival instinct?**

In horror movies, some individuals run and hide, and others stand up and fight. The fighters are the ones to survive, as they not only protect themselves but others around them. I'm curious why we are built this way. I believe it's a natural instinct. "According to Harvard Health Publishing, the flight or fight response evolved as a survival mechanism. When the human brain sensed danger, it triggered stress hormones that initiated physiological changes to prepare the body to either get away from the danger (flight) or fight it."(LeWine,MD, 2024)

Navigating Crushing Seasons
During my crushing season, I cried out to the Lord for help. I had a desire to respond in a negative way after discovering more details about Patrice's transition. It's natural to respond negatively, especially when you feel betrayed and have a sense of injustice. However, retaliation can make the pain and anger worse. Therefore, I had to think about what would bring peace and healing in this situation since there

was so much at stake. I did a lot of praying, crying, and seeking wise counsel through my spiritual family in Christ. I also consulted a therapist during this time. The bottom line in terms of what worked for me and how I continue to navigate this season is to surrender my will to the will of my Savior and trust Him.

For me, surrendering meant saying yes to the Lord despite what I was going through. I said yes to the Lord when I was in pain. I said yes to the Lord when I did not have the answers. I said yes to the Lord when my marriage was failing. I said yes to the Lord when my mother, father, and daughter transitioned…. I SAID YES!!!! Before saying yes, I asked the Lord what sets me apart in terms of what I've experienced and how I've made it to this point in my journey, and in my spirit, I felt the Lord saying, "You said YES" and I believe my yes have given me strength to walk with the Lord in crushing seasons. My yes gave me the power to overcome, fight for faith, and stay in the race. If you are not a believer, perhaps saying yes for you is simply continuing to live a purposeful life by staying true to your goals, plans, and who you are…

bottom line…your yes will be simply not to give up or throw in the towel in life.

 ### Will you say yes to the Lord while you're in the midst of the storm and rain?

As I wrap up this chapter, I am reminded of the processes of grief, not in any order because the emotions can change from day to day and from one moment to the next. The five stages of grief are: denial anger, bargaining, depression, and acceptance (Kubler-Ross, Kessler 2014), and no one person processes them the same way. The emotions that come with grief can be debilitating if it is not acknowledged and dealt with. I acknowledge that even today, as I write the story of my daughter Patrice, my family and I are still processing and healing. We miss her during special events, holidays, birthdays, and simply from day to day. Patrice and I spoke almost daily and when too much time would go by, I'd reach out to her to see how she and my grandchildren were doing.

Life has not been the same without my beautiful Patrice. My family and I continue to create what many call a "new normal," but I must admit that it's not easy. Her three beautiful children continue to thrive, live, and heal, and for that, we are grateful!!! Patrice's memory is forever etched in our hearts. If you are in a season of grief, know that you never have to do it alone. Reach out, ask for help, and seek counseling support if needed. By doing so, you can both heal and thrive at the same time.

Isaiah 43:2 NLT: When you pass through the waters, I will be with you; and when you pass through the rivers, they will not sweep over you. When you walk through the fire, you will not be burned; the flames will not set you ablaze.

Journal

_____

_____

_____

_____

_____

_____

_____

_____

_____

_____

_____

_____

_____

_____

_____

_____

_____

_____

_____

_____

CHAPTER 4

Why Are We Crushed

When reflecting on why we are crushed, it is more of a feeling about the emotional weight and pain we carry than a literal sense of being crushed. Oftentimes, it's the events that happen to us or to those we love and care about, including things that are out of our control, that make us feel like we are being crushed. Have you heard the term "crushed dreams"? It means having a beautiful hope and something terrible takes it away, like it never existed. More like someone just stepped on it and crushed it brutally.

Why are we Crushed is a question similar to why bad things happen to good people. It's really a question about our finite state or limits in our ability as human beings. It's hard to understand and imagine why things happen in our lives that cause excruciating pain and discomfort. Who really wants to feel pain? Who wakes up saying, I think I'd like to experience grief on a level that can shake my very core? Absolutely no one with a healthy mind because most human beings want to see good things happen, be free of pain and discomfort, experience joy and peace, and have a harmonious life. However, we are living in a "fallen" world, which means there will be pain and discomfort along the way.

 **What are the issues and circumstances in your life leading you to ask the question: Why?**

Fallen Nature of Man

According to research by licensed counselor, Kenya Crawford-Walker, there are three areas that generational curses manifest: genetically, environmentally, and spiritually.

Some of the pain and crushing we have experienced in life has much to do with the fall of man, but what do the terms "Fallen World" and

"Fallen Nature" actually mean? I'm glad you asked. We briefly discussed this in previous chapters; however, I want to expound on this topic since most of the pain and hardship in life is partly due to this reason, thus producing falling people with falling natures. In Romans 3:23 KJV, the scripture reads, "We have all sinned and fallen short of the glory of God." What do *we have all sinned* mean?

Genesis 3:1-19 is the story of how the fallenness of man began. It's a story of the deceiver (Satan) gaining entrance into the lives of humans by deceptions of their own desires and *curiosity*. That's where it all began in terms of the fallenness of man and is applicable to today ...sin is birthed through a desire acted upon. This is why scripture Eph 4:26 KJV says, be angry but sin not. In The Message version reads: Ephesians4:26-27MSG [26-27] Go ahead and be angry. You do well to be angry—but don't use your anger as fuel for revenge. *And don't stay angry.* Don't go to bed angry. *Don't give the Devil* that kind of foothold in your life. I appreciate the Message version as it speaks to being angry as a normal emotion, but acting on it is when we fall short.

Before Cain killed his brother Able, the Lord warned Cain (Genesis 4:7), saying, "*Sin is at your door*," if he did not heed the voice of the Lord... He knew Cain's "desire," and his desire caused him to sin. James 1:14-16 GNT reads: "But we are tempted when we are drawn away and trapped by our own evil desires. Then our evil desires conceive and give birth to sin, and sin, when it is full-grown, gives birth to death. Do not be deceived, my dear friends!" We see here that the fallenness of man begins with an internal complete that manifests externally when acted upon.

The Book of Psalms 51:5AMP reads, "*I was brought forth in [a state of] wickedness; In sin my mother conceived me [and from my beginning I, too, was sinful]*." Through the fall of man, sin interfered with the world; and thus caused humans to experience evil. This is why we do not have to teach children to do wrong; it's a natural instinct... the sinful nature, a natural born *curiosity* and bent towards sin. No one has to teach a child how to lie, steal, or cheat... No one had to teach me how to take puffs of a cigarette when no one was looking... no one had to show me how to steal liquor and drink it on my way to school. It's inherited! Sin was passed on from generation to generation; where we have heard the term 'generational curses,' which are sins passed from one generation to the other. Here is what the Old Testament scriptures tell us about generational curses:

Exodus 20:5-6NIV reads, 5: *"You shall not bow down to them or worship them; for I, the Lord your God, am a jealous God, punishing the children for the sin of the parents to the third and fourth generation of those who hate me, 6 but showing love to a thousand generations of those who love me and keep my commandments"*.

Exodus 34: 6-7NIV reads, "6 And he passed in front of Moses, proclaiming, *The Lord, the Lord, the compassionate and gracious God, slow to anger, abounding in love and faithfulness, 7 maintaining love to thousands, and forgiving wickedness, rebellion, and sin. Yet he does not leave the guilty unpunished; he punishes the children and their children for the sin of the parents to the third and fourth generation."*

Bishop Dale Bronner writes, "A generational curse does not mean you are automatically in the generational curses; it means there is a weakness or predisposition towards that generational curse or sin. This means you must be careful when indulging in alcohol if alcoholism runs in the family (Bronner 2024 Delivered).

 ### What areas of your life do you see generational sins playing out?

Here are some descriptions of what are considered generational curses, which can reportedly manifest in three ways:

Genetics: physical illness i.e., diabetes, cancer, high blood pressure, dementia, etc. Are mostly caused by family history, like high blood pressure or cancer. This is one of the reasons why physician's questions are associated with your family's medical condition: to determine if some of what you are experiencing is related. For example, my father's side of the family has a history of cancer, and my mother also had cancer. Therefore, my doctor is intentional about my annual exams and even started exams that are typically provided later in life, early as preventative medicine. According to the American Cancer

Society, 5 - 10% of cancer is inherited, and the rest is lifestyle changes. Knowing this information gives me both education and tools to work with, and the same applies to you. Just because someone in your family has a particular disease does not automatically mean you will. However, it means you have the "predisposition" to do so (Crawford, 2011).

Environmental: poverty, broken relationships, divorce, imprisonment (father, sons, brothers in prison or been to prison), and destructive behaviors. The term "Intergenerational incarceration" means multiple members from the same family experience incarceration and sometimes at the same time. Like a father and son, both experiencing time in prison.

Supernatural: rebellion and disobedience, a form of hate towards God. Rebellion is the sin of witchcraft ...I King 15:23 *"For rebellion is as the sin of witchcraft, and stubbornness is as iniquity and idolatry."*

Over and over in the Bible, we see the children of Israel rebelling against the Lord. From collecting more manna (food) than they were instructed to (Exodus 16:20) to making a golden calf for an idol worship (Exodus 32:7–10) and more. The greatest one we see is what we discussed before about the fall of man. Adam received instructions to not eat the fruit of the tree, and he did so. We also see this example in everyday life when we are told not to do something by an employer, mentor, or someone in authority, yet we do what we're told not to do.

"These curses and their strongholds can be broken by prayer, faith, and by replacing destructive and ungodly behaviors with more positive constructive behaviors. This is also possible through psychoeducation and the application of principles that help one to create and maintain successful relationships. "Our Creator has given us the ability to choose blessings and curses" (Crawford, 2011).

 **What destructive behaviors do you see in your life or your family life?**

Since we talked about dysfunctional families, I thought it was also important to talk about some of the generational curses that are often linked with dysfunction. If you and I are going to come out, be free and healed, recognize the reason that is causing pain to be exposed, and resolve some level of the question of Why we are *Crushed*.

Sin has no power when it's exposed! Let me be more specific: the devil has no power when he is exposed! I am determined to let you know the source so that you can seek THE SOURCE... Our Lord and Savior Jesus Christ. He is truly the one who sets us free. John 8:36 NIV states, "*So if the son (The Lord Jesus) sets you free, you will be free indeed.*" In the context of my daughter's passing, I was devastated and did not want to endure the process, nor did I want to take the time to explain to the people who asked about her. I also had to deal with the thought of serving my Lord, being a minister of the Gospel, and yet experiencing the loss of a child. How can I be an effective minister for the Lord, considering what's happened in my life? Who would even listen to me? I thought that I was exempt from this sort of pain and believed I would see my daughter's total deliverance and healing.

There were even thoughts of what I did wrong. Is there something I could have done to prevent this from happening I prayed for Patrice's deliverance and healing daily. I was even given a dream to go pray with her for deliverance, and I did, but maybe I should have prayed harder, longer, and more intently…These are some of the questions I had to wrestle with. In addition to all of this, someone even went as far as to say, "Your so-called god, let this happen." I questioned "Why" but did not blame God as I reminded myself of the scripture mentioned in Job: 1:22, "In all of this, Job did not sin by blaming God." Am I, at times, broken and filled with grief? Absolutely, just as Job was. As with the Book of Job, we will end well if we keep our eyes on Jesus. You and I may not have all the answers or know why, but God does, and that's enough for me.

What I know is that God is sovereign, and He loves us. I was homeless and lost everything, and God brought me out through deliverance and with a mighty hand! So, for me, it's hard to blame someone who loves you and has proven to you over the years how much He loves you. Now, I have cried out in agony and pain to my Lord while laying at his feet giving him all the hurt, disappointment, and pain. In turn, I am comforted with His presence…

Isaiah61:3NKJV *"To console those who mourn in Zion, To give them beauty for ashes, The oil of joy for mourning, The garment of praise for the spirit of heaviness; That they may be called trees of righteousness, The planting of the Lord, that He may be glorified."*

Strengthening Our Resolve

One of the terms used frequently by Bishop Lafayette Scales during our times of prayer is "May the Lord Strengthen our Resolve," which is something that we must do when it comes to thinking about why we are crushed. So, let's explore what this means so we can have an idea of what we need to do about these seasons of uncertainty. The word "strengthen," according to the Oxford Dictionary, means to "make or become stronger." and resolve means to "settle or find a solution, i.e., a problem, dispute, or a contentious matter." I also take strengthening our resolve to prevent "being mentally tormented," causing an increase in anguish, depression, oppression, and stagnation. Therefore, we must settle in on what we know is true and sure. After doing this, we find peace in our hearts and minds that we have done everything we can to make sense of our situation, and when it doesn't make sense, trusting that God has a plan.

Trusting God is what gives me hope and peace. I hope it does the same for you. I know there are some things that are hard to grapple with because of our own limitations. As human beings, we have limited ability to know things, but serving God, who is All Knowing, makes a difference. With that in mind, here is what I have done to strengthen my resolve: I have concluded that I did everything I could to help my daughter live a different lifestyle and life. I prayed over her, prayed for her, prayed with her, gave, supported, encouraged, and loved her through her process. God also graced me to demonstrate a new way of living. The unfortunate moments that changed her very existence from this life to the next are something that was out of my control. Now, is my conclusion helpful with the pain of losing a child? Absolutely not. Therefore, I hold strongly to my conviction, and prayerfully, you will hold strong to yours... besides, not every negative, painful experience that hits your life has anything to do with what "you did or did not do." My prayer as we move forward is that we don't forget the people we love, but that we release the grip of self-condemnation. I also pray that we are as kind to ourselves as we are to others.

 **Is there anything in your life you need to strengthen your resolve on?**

For the unbeliever, this may be an opportunity to explore Christianity and put your trust in a power higher than you. This is extremely helpful in terms of managing any type of grief and sorrow you've experienced in your crushing seasons. Here are some steps to take to accept the Lord Jesus Christ into your heart and to allow Him to be on the seat of your emotions; making him the Lord of your life; which is done by praying a prayer of repentance, which means to feel or express sincere regret or remorse about one's wrongdoing or sin (oxford dictionary) and asking Jesus into your heart. For example:

"Lord, I come to you acknowledging that I am a sinner in need of a Savior. I ask that you forgive me of my sins and receive me as yours. Thank you for being my Savior, in Jesus Name Amen!

If you are not connected to a local church, please do so for continued growth, connection, accountability, and support.

I would love to have given you a straightforward answer on why we are crushed, but what I can say is we can overcome, grow, and learn from our experience, as well as share the hope we have with others, letting them know that they too can overcome and heal. And guess what…it's a journey. There will be times of exuberant joy and times when you feel heavy-hearted, but I want you to know that you can do this! You can do the impossible. There is hope and we will talk more about this in Chapter 8.

Journal

_____

_____

_____

_____

_____

_____

_____

_____

_____

_____

_____

_____

_____

_____

_____

_____

_____

_____

_____

CHAPTER 5

Finding Purpose

Finding purpose in life is something we all hope for and seek. There are times you might question your presence and existence especially when you are trying to find a purpose in the chaotic, crushing season. We will explore this topic through life application, experience, and examples and provoke a desire to look within to see your purpose.

My husband and I were separated for 9 months. We went through a serious trial. Our conflicted relationship had many bumps that led us to separation. As a result, there were talks of divorce and we even went as far as to receive counsel from attorneys. One of the things that we did was meet with our Pastor and we submitted to wise counsel as well. He uses foolish things as the scripture says, to confound the wise (I Corinthians 1:27 NIV). Little did I know, God had a plan to use this crushing season for His purpose.

I presented the information to my pastor, and we explored the topic further by choosing a book to help guide the group, which was "The Power of the Praying Wife" by Stormy Omartian. The group was later developed, and a core group of sisters came alongside me, whom I'd been friends with for 20-plus years. The group is called the Virtuous Wife's Prayer Ministry, which was launched in 2014 with a vision to support wives in their roles. Through the ministry, God Has enabled me to minister and support wives in their roles by creating a loving safe space for confidential conversation and exploration through God's Word. While the ministry has evolved over the years, we continue to meet regularly and provide ongoing support to this day.

Did it take a separation from my husband and almost the end of a marriage to birth the virtuous wife's prayer ministry? Could the ministry have come forward without an 'almost failed' marriage? I cannot answer these questions, but what I can say is that God used this trial, this tragedy or near tragedy, as an opportunity to birth forth purpose. What the enemy meant for evil, God worked it not only for good, but for a purpose. In Genesis 50:20 NLT it reads, "You intended to harm me, but God intended it for good" which was spoken by Joseph when his own brothers set a trap for him to bring him harm. Though Joseph experienced tragedy, he was raised to triumph and was used to save the ones who harmed him.

 **In what ways can God use you right now to help others with the thing that you are struggling with or has caused you pain?**

Tragedy to Triumph

Throughout the world, there are individuals going from "Tragedy to Triumph." As a matter of fact, while doing my research on this topic, I discovered over 25 million entries on the subject matter. But what does this actually mean? There are multiple individuals who have experienced some sort of tragedy or crushing in their lives and somehow found purpose in their pain. II Corinthians 2:14 KJV, it reads, *"Now thanks be unto God, which always causeth us to triumph in Christ, and maketh manifest the savour of his knowledge by us in every place."* There are seasons for sackcloth and ashes, which are painfully crushing, and there are seasons to anoint yourself and wash your face which actually heal and refresh your mind and spirit. *In any season of our lives the purpose is still the purpose and must be fulfilled.*

I read a quote by D. W. Journals that said, "God Often Uses Our Deepest Pain As the Launching Pad of Our Greatest Calling." Now, note the words from Romans 8:28, *"All things work together for the good of them that love God and are called according to HIS PURPOSE!"* What I gather from this is the fact that our pain is used as a purpose, like a catapult or launch pad, which is something that provides you with the opportunity to follow a particular plan of action. It was the fuel that lit the spark, kindling the flame. No, God did not cause it…. He USED IT!!! There is nothing wasted in the Kingdom!

There is something about escaping hell that burns in us a zeal to be better, do better, and perhaps it's a little nudge to push us into our next. For some of us, it's hard to see the light at the end of the tunnel or the bright side of things. To be able to see the light easily, you need to be a little bent on optimism. However, when there is more of a bent to pessimism, there is more of a sense of doom and gloom. How you see your situation is pivotal in how you move forward in finding your purpose.

 **Do you think crushing seasons can be used as fuel to light the fire within?**

The Treasure Within

Once my mother planned to nominate me for a community volunteer award. She sent me an email asking me to fill out this form and to make a list of all my accomplishments, and I did not have anything to add… at least I didn't think so at that time. I did not feel like I was a person that was worthy of this community award. I didn't feel like what I did mattered much, and I wasn't sure exactly how to document what I did. So, I sent a message back to my mom saying, "I do not have anything to write, and I don't know what to say." In turn, she responded, "You are successful, and give yourself some credit…you have accomplished a lot." I did not see my accomplishments, but my mother did, and sometimes it takes someone from the outside to help us see the things within us that are more precious than gold, and what is in you is tied to your purpose. Whatever you are passionate about is an indication that it may very well be your purpose.

You and I have a reservoir of *treasure* inside of us! Let's search for that *treasure* and see what we find. Remember, we come from good stock

- But you are God's chosen *treasure* —priests who are kings, a spiritual "nation" set apart as God's devoted ones. He called you out of darkness to experience his marvellous light, and now he claims you as his very own (1 Peter 2:9-10 TPT)

- God has chosen you to be a people for himself, a special *treasure* above all the peoples who are on the face of the earth Deuteronomy 14:2 (KJV).

You may be thinking, what is my purpose, and how can I find it? Many of you are walking in your purpose and may need to solidify that your current work, ministry, volunteerism, and support you provide to others may very well be your purpose. Others may not see their purpose or think they have one. However, we ALL have a PURPOSE. This is the reason something is done, created, or exists, as one's intention or objective (Oxford Dictionary). Oswald Chambers said, "As Christians, we are not here for our own purpose at all. We are here for the purpose of God, and the two are not the same (Chambers, 2022). I've also heard it said that your "Why" is your purpose.

 **What keeps you up at night? What angers you when you see or hear something that sparks a desire for justice and equality?**

Many organizations and groups were birthed out of purpose and desire to bring change to the lives of others who were struggling the same way. I am a witness that whatever you may be dealing with today may be a direct link to your purpose. Continue to explore, seek wise counsel, and look deep within. Remember, when you help others, you, too, are helped! Find your purpose and flourish!

Journal

CHAPTER 6

Resilience

Resilience is the key to conquer and overcome during crushing seasons. God made us to be resilient. He has placed His Spirit within us, which introduces a "bounce back" mentality from tragedy, upsets, letdowns, and brokenness.

When I think about my life, I think about how I have made it this far, and I'm sure you have had the same thoughts when you look back over your own life. What do you attribute your progress to, or to who? I can say that God is the number one factor in sustaining power in my life. He is the one that has kept and continues to keep me. The other contributing factors are my connections to people and the prayer warriors that I've had in my life.

These are the people I know and I love—those who have been a part of my life, stood by my side, and prayed for me during my hardest moments. Their resiliency increased my level of resiliency. Resiliency is contagious.

 **Have you observed resiliency in someone you know?**

What is Resiliency?

Resiliency is something that helps you move forward despite adversity. It is something that is developed within and gives you the power to overcome during crushing seasons. Resiliency rises within and causes us to triumph in adversity. It is the "ability to bend without breaking, to hold steady when a gale-force of stressor threaten stability, to remain curious through the confusion and energized by uncertainty" (Hull, 2023). The uncertainty of moving forward while experiencing crushing seasons is a brave and powerful move. Therefore, we want to lean in and build the resiliency muscle!

What does resilience mean? The Oxford Dictionary states that *resilience is the capacity to withstand or to recover quickly from difficulties; toughness and the ability of a substance or object to spring back into shape; elasticity*. It's also said to be "the result of a complex series of internal and external characteristics, including genetics, physical fitness, mental health, and environment" (Walker et al, 2017).

Therefore, what we can gather from the meaning provided is that there are benefits of building up our level of resiliency to empower us to heal and grow!

 **What is one thing you can do today to increase your level of resiliency?**

Resiliency in Trauma

Resiliency is said to be a protective factor and is impacted by "coping mechanisms, upbringing, support systems, education, environment, and our belief system. However, "resilience may be a major protective factor required for an adaptive response of an individual in stressful situations..." (Kocjan et al, 2021)

Let's discuss this topic in the context of global traumatic events that are closely connected to grief and assault, such as racism, 911, and the impacts of the COVID-19 pandemic. During any life-altering event, we choose to fight or flight as mentioned in Chapter 3. However, this is also the aspect of resilience in responding to these events, and it's important to remember that how someone chooses to respond should never be judged by others in any way.

Do you know that some people will question how you are over the death of a loved one because they do not understand the way you respond to grief or how you have chosen to cope with a tragic event in your life?

I am surprised when I hear about such things because no one shares the same experience and walks away with the same outcome. For example, during the first year of my daughter's transition, I would cry every morning before going to work during my devotional time.

On rainy days, the pain seemed to intensify as I remembered how she was pulled out of a car and left on the ground in the rain before the coroner picked her up. Something else happened to me physically during this time...it appeared as though I had a heart attack, according to a cardiologist. I went through a battery test and had to wear a heart monitor for 30 days.

In my heart, I knew it was not a heart attack... I was simply suffering from the pain and grief of losing my daughter. I later learned of the term "Broken Heart Syndrome," which occurs during severe emotional or physical stress" (LeWine, 2024). Therefore, I have concluded that not all grief or trauma requires an audience or an answer...it just simply is.

If you and I are not responding well to life's challenges, it doesn't mean we're weak; it simply means there are opportunities to strengthen our core, which is like ab exercises. "Think of your core muscles as the sturdy central link in a chain connecting your upper and lower body. Whether you're hitting a tennis ball or mopping the floor, the necessary motions either originate in your core or move through it (Harvard Publishing, 2024)."

Building resilience is like building your core muscles, enabling you to rise from difficult seasons. The same with a strong core that enables you to stand tall, a strong core of resilience can help reduce your stress and empower you to deal with painful emotions.

Growing in Resilience

If you lack resilience, it's not too late to learn and grow in this area of your life. According to the Harvard University article on the Science of Resilience, "The brain and other biological systems are most adaptable early in life. Yet, while their development lays the foundation for a wide range of resilient behaviors, it is *never too late to build resilience.* Age-appropriate, health-promoting activities can significantly improve the odds that an individual will recover from stress-inducing experiences. For example, regular physical exercise, stress-reduction practices, and programs that actively build executive function and self-regulation skills can improve the abilities of children and adults to cope with, adapt to, and even prevent adversity in their lives. Adults who strengthen these skills in themselves can better model healthy behaviors for their children, thereby improving the resilience of the next generation". (Center on Developing Child, 2015).

We need to be resilient to cope with uncertainty and surprises. For example, during the onset of the pandemic crisis, countries around the globe increased self-care and precautionary measures due to the traumatic outbreak and also because there were some risk factors involved with being infected with COVID-19. Now those who were 65 years or older and had chronic medical conditions like COPD, heart disease, and obesity were more inclined to get exposed to the virus (Center for Disease Control, 2024). Many of us did not even know how to cope with the changing events. Self-care is a part of resilience, finding ways to cope during a traumatic event. Almost everyone, including me, changed our diets, increased our exercise, and made self-care a priority.

Self-care is a part of resilience, which is essential to cope during a traumatic event. In the crushing season of the pandemic, the number of deaths and grief, along with isolation, was insurmountable. Families struggled, and the idea of socialization we knew had come to a halt. The level of comfort we would typically offer individuals during a significant loss had changed. We had to show our love from afar. Some of us had loved ones who passed away or were admitted to hospitals in critical condition, but what we all experienced was an increase in social media use, which allowed us to socialize and show support in different ways. We had to build a community across social media, which is another aspect of resilience. We used this newfound way to share our pain, disappointments, joys, and emotions in a community where we could not only receive feedback but also support someone else. We were paving the way for resilience! Resilience is a part of our everyday life, and we need to tap into it daily to live the life of an overcomer.

In addition, we saw an increase and rise in racism. For example, George Floyd and the aftermath of his death caught on camera for the world to see. Many of us were affected by this loss. While some of us begin to experience an increased level of racism, others experience a variety of forms of microaggressions. It was as if the situation exposed itself, and individuals who had some racist views of other cultures became more visible.

I will say one of the forms of resilience that I can reflect on in terms of going through that season and being in social services is providing resources for individuals for counseling, which is a form of resilience as well. When you're consulting someone for emotional support to build coping skills, you are paving the road for resilience because we know that resiliency transforms potentially toxic stress into tolerable stress (Center on Developing Child,2015), which is the ultimate goal.

As we wrap up this chapter, I want to say that life experiences and crushing seasons can be extremely difficult to navigate alone. Please seek assistance if you are having difficulty. You do not have to live life alone!

Journal

_____

_____

_____

_____

_____

_____

_____

_____

_____

_____

_____

_____

_____

_____

_____

_____

_____

CHAPTER 7

You Were Built for this

You were built for the trials and tests you have gone through and experienced over the years. You were built for this!

No, you were not built to be abused, mistreated, or rejected. However, you were built to overcome and confront issues and address bad behaviors along with dysfunction that interfere with your progress. How can we appreciate the sun if it was never cloudy? How can we appreciate walking in victory if we have never experienced defeat? You were built for this and built to overcome, built to prosper, and built to walk in Victory!

It's taking me some time to realize that I was built to walk in victory, but doing so has empowered me, and I pray the same for you! I have learned to address issues related to dysfunctional behaviors with friends, family, and people I know and love. I have come to realize that these are difficult conversations, but remember, God has called us to do hard things, and we can do so courageously. I do not believe that He wants us to be doormats, to be used or abused by anyone. You are worthy of so much more than this if you have or are experiencing some form of abuse.

While steep in addiction, I was held against my will and physically assaulted. The pain and degradation left me feeling less than a person, which made me question my very existence. I remember going home with a busted lip and a bruised face covered under makeup.

 **What needs to be uncovered in your life so that you can be free? Expose it!**

Later in life, after my deliverance, I had an opportunity to see my perpetrator. I cannot explain how this happened. All I can say is that God created a path for me and gave me the strength to talk to him, which seemed impossible before. I was on one side of the street, and he was on another; we were both waiting for public transportation, and I recognized him from across the street in downtown Columbus; in the midst of all the people waiting to catch the bus, I saw him. The next thing I knew, I was standing right in front of him. Of course, I did not look like the same person, that I was years ago. However, I approached him, and the first thing I said was, "Do you remember me?" At first, he did not recognize me and stepped back. Then he looked again, and I could see in his eyes that he remembered me, and he acknowledged, "Yes, I remember you." What I said next shocked me, and I did not know how this would go. I said, "You hurt me, and I forgive you. I forgive you." He stood there and seemed to be in shock. I walked away and got on the bus with tears of relief.

Do you realize it was God who gave me the strength to confront this man who inflicted pain on my life? I did not know that I had the ability to do so. Believe it or not, there was no screaming, yelling, or swinging of the hands, which is something I thought I would do if I ever saw him again. However, I literally walked out the scripture in Joshua 1:9 NIV on this day… "Have I not commanded you? Be strong and courageous. Do not be afraid; do not be discouraged, for the LORD your God will be with you wherever you go".

 **What is God calling you to address that requires you to be Bold and Courageous?**

Along with being strong and courageous, I saw the gift of mercy in operation. This is a gift for those who are in need of God's mercy. "*Blessed are the merciful: for they shall obtain mercy*" (Matthew 5:7). "Mercy is what we express when we are led by God to be compassionate in our attitudes, words, and actions. It is more than feeling sympathy toward someone; it is love enacted. Mercy desires to answer the immediate needs of others and alleviate suffering, loneliness, and grief. Mercy addresses physical, emotional, financial, or spiritual crises with generous, self-sacrificial service. Mercy is a champion of the lowly, poor, exploited, and forgotten and often acts on their be-half." (My Spiritual Gifts, 2024)

God created us, and He is the expert who knows us more than we know about ourselves or others. Like a trainer: Oh, I remember having mine, who pushed me to go beyond my limits just for the sake of my very well-being. When I thought 10 lbs was the heaviest weight my body could bear, he handed me 20, and guess what? I was able to lift his recommended weights. Perhaps there is something within that wants to take the easy route; you know the shortcut. However, doing so produces very little lasting results. Oftentimes, to see results, we must increase our load, and more repetitions can be completed. We can do more than we think...

I have seen countless examples of this, even in Church. Like when we lift our hands up in the sky... And then the minister would say stretch a little further... And guess what? Some are able to stretch while others cannot. The question afterward is why we did not stretch as far as we could when we were asked to initially. See, the exercise proves the individuals have the ability and capacity to do more and were BUILT to stretch further but needed a little coaching and encouragement to do so.

Rebuild!

There are times when you and I may need to rebuild our lives on a firm foundation for safe navigation through the crushing seasons. Our lives may have been built on shallow ground, lacking substance and the ability to stand firm when the storms of life are raging, increasing the likelihood of being washed up even at the slight storm. What we need to do is fortify and fill the holes that may cause us not to respond well. Remember, you were built for this… but what did we build our lives, marriages, friendships, business relationships, careers, ministries, and aspirations on?

A home built on low-grade or bad materials requires frequent, costly repairs, and the owner must decide between frequent repairs and rebuilding (Wallender, 2022). In the book of Matthew 7: 24-27, there is a picture of a house standing or falling based on the foundation. One was built on solid rock, and the other on sand. The scripture correlates the way each house was built based on those who listened and followed the Word of God. Those who listened to God had their house withstand the storms, but the ones who disobeyed had their houses built on sand, and the wind blew away their shelters.

Before my life with Christ and even in my early walks with Him, my life was like a house built on sand because I did not know the Word of God, lacked trust, and honestly did not have the mind or know how to stand when experiencing life's crushing seasons. Therefore, I had to learn how to live and *rebuild* my foundation so that I could face the storm. Here are some of the things that I did and do to *rebuild* a firm foundation in my life:

- Pray daily.

- Listen and read the Word daily.

- Connect with a Bible-believing Church.

- Connect with spiritual-minded individuals that will hold you accountable.

- Seek wise counsel through the counsel of the Holy Spirit and counsel from a church, mentor, or counselor.

- Take Personal Development courses to facilitate growth and healing: (ex., *Breakthrough ministry classes, deliverance ministry classes, gift discovery classes, leadership ministry, discipleship training, understanding God, college courses, and more.*)

 **What are some things you can do today to start the rebuilding process in your life if needed?**

Journal

_____

_____

_____

_____

_____

_____

_____

_____

_____

_____

_____

_____

_____

_____

_____

_____

_____

_____

_____

CHAPTER 8

The Hope

"I wouldn't trade anything for my journey" is highly quoted and used in songs and poetry and was originally inspired by Maya Angelou. My journey has led me to a place in my life where I can appreciate and value the process that made me the strong person I am today. Would I have liked some of the processing to speed up so I could move to the next juncture in life? Absolutely! However, there are no quick ways to go through the process of crushing seasons. The lessons and wisdom that are the by-products of your experience will be lasting, though the crushing is only for a moment...but it can feel like a lifetime. The process is very similar to making a diamond.

The Sparkle

When we look at a diamond, we see the beauty it holds, the bling, the shine, and the glitter, which is eye-catching and causes everyone who sees it to look twice and stand in awe of the results of heat and pressure applied. We like the results of this heat and pressure applied to make such a beautiful piece of jewelry, but the process of making a diamond is a long, intense process. We want the *sparkle*, but we do not want the process.

For example, I was a high-school dropout who desired to go back to school to get my diploma (the *sparkle*). Well, after dropping out of school, getting my GED was not easy, and I had to take the test twice and pass it on the second try. The first time I took the test without preparing and studying...I wanted the sparkle but not the process. Next, I wanted a college degree and went to college for an Associate in Business Management. It was not easy, but I pressed through the grueling process to reach my goal. I decided to go back to school for a Bachelor's in Psychology, and again, I found the process to be extremely difficult. By now, you know what I wanted...the *sparkle* without the process.

I went back to school again for a Master's in Social Work and almost fainted and gave up many times. Often, I asked myself, "*Why am I doing this again?*" but there was a greater purpose in mind. So, I continued the process, gave dedication, and eventually got my *sparkle*... Anything we want to last will require hard work and dedication. Things might get tough with time and even uncomfortable, but remember, we get the sparkle only after staying consistent.

 **What have you delayed completing due to the requirements to make your desire a reality?**

While researching how diamonds are made, I learned that original diamonds were made billions of years ago under 100 miles below the earth's surface. These precious stones were made from the crystallization of carbon atoms under extreme heat and pressure (Lineberry, 2024). In fact, the research goes on to say that the only way to receive such precious jewels is for there to be a "volcanic eruption," which causes the diamonds to rise to the surface from the upper mantle of the earth (Lineberry, 2024). So, the process of making a diamond is vigorous, with direct pressure and heat. The same goes for our lives; just like a diamond, we need to go through a process. Though painful, keep pushing. When it feels like the walls are crashing down around you, Do not lose hope!

 **Do you see the correlation between the diamond and life's processes?**

Choose Hope

In every season of life, crushing or seasons of victory, we can still have hope, which is not a mere feeling; it is a *knowing and a state of being*! We have to have hope, make efforts, and believe in ourselves every single day. Do you know that many individuals go to work, serve in ministry, and volunteer; because they believe that their work brings hope to someone? Furthermore, I would say doing so also increases their hope and joy by giving back to others. In the Book of Luke 6:38AMP, the scripture is often associated with financial giving in the church. However, it also speaks of giving in your efforts and deeds. It reads: "Give, and it will be given to you. They will pour into your lap a good measure—pressed down, shaken together, and running over [with no space left for more]. For with the standard of measurement you use *[when you do good to others]*, it will be measured to you in return." The scripture speaks to the reciprocity of serving and helping others. The giver also receives hope!

 Do you find it hard to choose hope? If so, what is one thing you can do to move towards a more hopeful attitude and mindset?

Hope is a choice! It is more than a feeling. Hope is a choice that we make daily by saying:

- I am worth it…
- I will continue…
- I will keep moving forward...
- I will not give up on myself…
- I will not give up on my goals…
- I will keep fulfilling my purpose, regardless of how I feel.

Hope and Faith

Hope takes a measure of faith to believe; both faith and hope create the desire to overcome the crushing seasons. Hope says, "I think I can make it," and faith says, "Yes, you can." In order to have hope, faith must exist. Hence, the definition of hope: "Hope is a favorable and confident expectation; it is an expectant attitude that something good is going to happen and things will work out, no matter what situation we are facing" (Meyer, 2024).

In addition, there is something called *Hope Theory*, developed, and researched over a 30-year span of time by psychologist Charles R. Snyder. He wrote, "Hope is a dynamic motivational experience that is interactively derived from two distinct types of cognitive tools in the context of goal achievement—namely, pathways and agency thinking" (Snyder et al., 2017). Is hope a way of thinking, or is faith? The answer is both! On a daily basis, we choose faith by renewing our minds and thinking positively, even in crushing seasons.

Today, I want you to know that God created a reservoir of hope in each of us. I know, sometimes it does not feel like it, yet it is true. Jeremiah 29:11 NIV reads: *"For I know the plans I have for you, says the Lord, plans to do you good and not evil, plans to give you a future and a hope!"* The Hebrew word for Hope in this scripture is 'expectancy' and 'an expected end' in other versions of the scripture. Therefore, you and I can take comfort in knowing God's plans for our lives will prevail. I want to encourage you not to give up hope. You have come too far to give up now!

May you continue to overcome all things in every season...., especially in crushing seasons!

Romans 15:13 NIV - May the God of hope fill you with all joy and peace as you trust in him, so that you may overflow with hope by the power of the Holy Spirit.

Journal

Resources

**If you need counselling or need help in overcoming any crisis, here are a few resources to help you on your journey:

Church Finder (https://www.churchfinder.com/)

988 is a Suicide and Crisis Line (https://988lifeline. org/chat/)

Psychology Today is a free online resource to aide in search of counselor near you (https://www. psychologytoday.com/us)

Mental Health America offers free online and training resources. (https://mhanational.org/)

NAMI (National Alliance on Mental Illness) 62640 (Text) or call 800-950-6264 (https://www.nami. org/)

References

Bronner, B. C. (2024, Feb 11). Retrieved from Word of Faith Family Worship Cathedral.

Center for Disease Control. (2024, June 24). People with Certain Medical Conditions and COVID-19 Risk Factors. Retrieved from https://www.cdc.gov/covid/risk-factors/index.html

Center on Developing Child . (2015). The Science of Resilience (InBrief). Retrieved from Harvard University Center of: www.developingchild.harvard.edu.

Center on the Developing Child. (2024, August 22). The Science of Resilience. Retrieved from www.developingchild.harvard.edu.

Chambers, O. (2022, August 22). What does the Bible Say about Purpose. Retrieved from Bible Reasons: https://biblereasons.com/bible-verses-about-purpose/

Crawford, K. L. (2011). Overcoming Generational Curses. Retrieved from The Glory Magazine Page: https://perspective-counseling.com/files/2015/12/Overcoming-Generational-Curses-Pg.-45.pdf

Dictionary, O. (2024, August 22). Oxford Learners Dictionary. Retrieved from https://www.oxfordlearnersdictionaries.com/definition/english/capacity

Hadid, Y. (2024, August 22). Yolanda Hadid Quotes. (n.d.). BrainyQuote.com. . Retrieved from BrainyQuote.com : https://www.brainyquote.com/quotes/yolanda_hadid_872007

Harvard Publishing. (2024, August 22). The Real-World Benefits of Strengthening you Core. Retrieved from Harvard Health Publishing: https://www.health.harvard.edu/healthbeat/the-real-world-benefits-of-strengthening-your-core

Hull, D. (2023). The Realm of Resiliency. Prime Connections, 28-29.

Kocjan et al, G. Z. (2021). Resilience Matters: Explaining the Association between Personality and Psychological Functioning During the COVID-19 Pandemic. International Journal of Clinical and Health Psychology 21.

LeWine, MD, H. E. (2024, April 3). Understanding the Stress Response. Retrieved from Harvard Health Publishing: https://www.health.harvard.edu/staying-healthy/understanding-the-stress-response

Lineberry, C. (2024, August 22). Diamonds Unearthed. Retrieved from Smithsonian: https://www.smithsonianmag.com/science-nature/diamonds-unearthed-141629226/

Meyer, J. (2024, August 22). Living with Hope that Never Disappoints. Retrieved from Joyce Meyer Ministries: https://joycemeyer.org/grow-your-faith/articles/living-with-hope-that-never-disappoints

Mphaphuli, L. K. (2023). The Impact of Dysfunctional Families on the Mental Health of Children. Parenting in Modern Societies, 2-16.

My Spiritual Gifts. (2024). Mercy. Retrieved from My Spiritual Gifts: https://myspiritualgifts. com/spiritual-gifts/mercy.

Snyder et al, C. (2017). Hope Theory: A Member of the Positive Psychology Family. The Oxford Handbook of Hope, 27-44.

Stallone, S. (Director). (2006). Rocky Balboa [Motion Picture].

The Cycle of Intergenerational Incarceration. (2024). Retrieved from Interrogating Justice: https://interrogatingjustice.org/

Three Things to know about your Family History and Cancer Risk. (2024, April 5). Retrieved from American Cancer Society: https://www. fightcancer.org/three-things-know-about-your-family-history-and-cancer-risk

Walker et al, F. (2017). In the Search for Integrative Biomarker of Resilience to Psychological Stress. Neurosci Biobehave, 310-320.

Wallender, L. (2022, November 07). Should I Rebuild a House or Remodel a House. Retrieved from The Spruce: https://www.thespruce.com/remodel-or-tear-down-rebuild-your-house-1822447